VHF Yachtmaster

VHF YACHTMASTER

Pat Langley-Price & Philip Ouvry

ADLARD COLES
8 Grafton Street, London W1

Adlard Coles
William Collins Sons & Co. Ltd
8 Grafton Street, London W1X 3LA

First published in Great Britain by
Adlard Coles Ltd 1984
Reprinted 1988

British Library Cataloguing in Publication Data
Langley-Price, Pat
VHF yachtmaster.
1. Radio on boats
I. Title   II. Ouvry, Philip
623.8′5641   VM325

ISBN 0-229-11720-1

Typeset by Columns of Reading
Printed and bound in Great Britain by
Mackays of Chatham Limited, Kent

Contents

Acknowledgements

The authors wish to thank the following for help and encourage-
ment received in producing this textbook and the accompanying
cassette:

Her Majesty's Coastguard

British Telecom International (North Foreland Coast Radio
Station)

Thames Navigation Service (Gravesend Port Radio Station)

Merchant Navy Radio Operator Maurice Powell

Fisherman Ernie Stevens

Yachtsmen Huntley Strickland and Stan Garnet

Julian van Hasselt

Department of Transport, Marine Directorate (M notices)

Seafarer Navigation International Ltd

INTRODUCTION

Many small craft are now fitted with a VHF radio telephone. To use such a radio telephone a *Restricted Certificate of Competence in Radio Telephony VHF Only* is needed which involves a test to ensure that the discipline required is understood before going live on the air. Many people freeze when first faced with the microphone and its press-to-transmit switch: the carefully prepared script seems to come out broken and confused.

This textbook and its accompanying cassette have been produced to help the aspiring operator to get over these nerves and become a fluent communicator. The textbook gives the correct standard procedures and explains the reasons for them. The cassette then gives examples on how these procedures might sound in practice.

It is emphasised that these procedures must always be followed in principle but may be abbreviated or modified once proper communication has been established, provided that they do not become ambiguous or that any of the standard rules are not broken.

The objective is to establish the communication link and pass the message in a clear and concise manner. Consideration for other users must be borne in mind at all times.

The layout of both book and cassette has been designed to outline the distress and emergency procedures first, then to continue with the more routine communications. It is highly desirable that all members of the crew should be aware of the distress and emergency procedures as these can be used without the need for the operator to have a *Certificate of Competence*.

Having listened to the cassette and absorbed the information in the textbook, the would-be radio operator should apply to a *Royal Yachting Association* (RYA) examination centre to arrange the test for the *Certificate of Competence*. (Names and addresses of these centres are given in Appendix VIII.) This test is a half-hour written paper followed by a straightforward practical exercise. A passport size photograph, an up-to-date passport or birth certificate, plus the appropriate fee will be required.

The authors hope that this book and cassette will enable the reader to get on the air and enable him to use the VHF radio telephone to communicate with friends and colleagues, as well as giving him the confidence that the most effective aid for distress and emergency can be used properly and efficiently.

VHF PROCEDURE

Distress

The distress signal MAYDAY indicates that a vessel is threatened by GRAVE and IMMINENT danger and requests IMMEDIATE ASSISTANCE. A distress call has priority over all other traffic and may only be sent with the authority of the master or person responsible for the distressed vessel.

Channel 16 is normally used for the distress call as it is constantly monitored by the Coastguard who (within UK waters) has prime responsibility for co-ordination of maritime search and rescue (SAR). However, in case of difficulties on Channel 16, any other channel may be used.

The word MAYDAY is the distress signal. This is used to alert all stations within range that a distress call and message are about to follow. During distress working, radio silence is automatically imposed on all stations in the area not concerned with the distress.

Transmitting a distress call

1. Check that the main power supply is on.
2. Switch the radio to maximum power and tune to Channel 16.
3. Depress the press-to-transmit switch on the microphone.
4. Speak clearly and slowly.

The call:
1. MAYDAY three times.
2. The words: THIS IS.
3. The vessel's name or call sign three times.

The message:
1. MAYDAY once and the vessel's name or call sign once.
2. The vessel's position as accurately as possible, either in latitude and longitude or as a true bearing and distance *from* a known geographical point.
3. The nature of the distress and the assistance required.
4. Any other relevant information (including the number of persons on board).
5. The invitation to reply: OVER.

If an immediate reply is not received, check the operation of the radio and repeat the call at regular intervals.

(The inclusion of the word YACHT in the example opposite indicates the type of vessel in distress.)

During distress working, all messages should begin with distress signal MAYDAY.

Distress
Channel 16

The call:
> MAYDAY MAYDAY MAYDAY
> THIS IS YACHT LINNET YACHT LINNET YACHT LINNET

The message:
> MAYDAY YACHT LINNET
> MY POSITION IS TWO ZERO SEVEN DEGREES LANDS END
>   LIGHTHOUSE FORTY MILES
> I AM SINKING AND NEED IMMEDIATE ASSISTANCE
> I HAVE FIVE PERSONS ON BOARD
> OVER

Acknowledging the Call

A vessel receiving a MAYDAY call who is able to render assistance is obliged by maritime law to do so.

A distress call is acknowledged as follows:
1. The distress signal MAYDAY once.
2. The name or call sign of the distressed vessel three times.
3. The name or call sign of the acknowledging vessel three times.
4. The words: RECEIVED MAYDAY.

and as soon as possible after this acknowledgment:
5. The distress signal MAYDAY once.
6. The name or call sign of the distressed vessel three times.
7. The name or call sign of the acknowledging vessel three times.
8. The position of the acknowledging vessel, the speed at which she is proceeding to the given position of the distressed vessel and her estimated time of arrival at that position.
9. The word OVER.

The distressed vessel should reply.

After acknowledgement, both vessels now stand by on Channel 16, in case further communication is necessary.

Acknowledging the Call
Channel 16

MAYDAY
YACHT LINNET YACHT LINNET YACHT LINNET
THIS IS YACHT SEAFINCH YACHT SEAFINCH YACHT
  SEAFINCH
RECEIVED MAYDAY

MAYDAY
YACHT LINNET YACHT LINNET YACHT LINNET
THIS IS YACHT SEAFINCH YACHT SEAFINCH YACHT
  SEAFINCH
I AM TWO MILES NORTH EAST OF YOU MY SPEED IS FIVE
  KNOTS MY ETA AT YOUR POSITION IS THIRTY MINUTES
  FROM NOW
STAND BY ON THIS CHANNEL
OVER

MAYDAY
YACHT SEAFINCH YACHT SEAFINCH YACHT SEAFINCH
THIS IS YACHT LINNET YACHT LINNET YACHT LINNET
UNDERSTOOD
STANDING BY ON CHANNEL SIXTEEN

Mayday Relay

It may be necessary under the following circumstances for a vessel to relay a distress message for another vessel:

1. When the distressed vessel cannot herself transmit a distress message.

2. When the rescue vessel or the controlling station deem further assistance is required.

3. When a vessel not able to render assistance hears an unacknowledged distress message.

A relayed distress message is prefixed with the words MAYDAY RELAY.

In the example opposite, yacht *MERMAIN* hears a distress message from yacht *JETTO*. She is too far away to render assistance so she waits to see if a reply is forthcoming. No reply is received so she acknowledges the message and informs yacht *JETTO* that she will re-broadcast the mayday.

The Coastguard reckons on acknowledging a mayday within 5 seconds, so the Coast Radio Station will wait 5 seconds before acknowledging (to give the Coastguard time to respond). Another yacht should therefore wait 30 seconds and, if no other acknowledgement is heard, acknowledge the mayday herself.

If a yacht sees another vessel displaying a distress signal or in apparent difficulty, she should immediately inform the Coastguard before investigating further. This message may be passed on Channel 67 after initial contact has been made on Channel 16. It will enable the Coastguard to alert the search and rescue services in case further action should be necessary.

Mayday Relay
Channel 16

MAYDAY RELAY MAYDAY RELAY MAYDAY RELAY
THIS IS YACHT MERMAIN YACHT MERMAIN YACHT
  MERMAIN
THE FOLLOWING RECEIVED FROM YACHT JETTO
BEGINS MAYDAY YACHT JETTO
CALL SIGN MIKE UNIFORM ECHO ALFA
POSITION ONE SIX FIVE LIZARD POINT THREE ZERO MILES
SINKING NEED IMMEDIATE ASSISTANCE
SIX PERSONS ON BOARD ENDS
OVER

Imposing Radio Silence

The station controlling the distress is one of the following:
1. The distressed vessel.
2. The vessel sending the relay.
3. Any other station which has assumed or had this authority delegated to it. (In United Kingdom waters the Coastguard automatically assumes this authority.)

If the controlling station deems it necessary to impose radio silence on any station interfering with the distress transmissions she will do so by transmitting a message containing the words SEELONCE MAYDAY. If a station other than the controlling station believes it is essential for her to impose radio silence the words SEELONCE DISTRESS should be used.

Relaxing Radio Silence

Channel 16 is used for initial calling and is therefore normally very busy. If radio silence is no longer vital the controlling station transmits a message which includes the word PRUDONCE. This means that essential transmissions may now be made.

Cancelling Radio Silence

When distress working is finished and radio silence is no longer necessary the controlling station transmits a message which includes the words SEELONCE FEENEE. This means that normal working can now resume.

Imposing Radio Silence
Channel 16

SEELONCE MAYDAY THIS IS FALMOUTH COASTGUARD
OUT

SEELONCE DISTRESS THIS IS YACHT MERMAIN
OUT

Relaxing Radio Silence
Channel 16

MAYDAY
ALL STATIONS ALL STATIONS ALL STATIONS
THIS IS FALMOUTH COASTGUARD
TIME ONE ONE ONE FIVE GMT
YACHT JETTO
PRUDONCE
OUT

Cancelling Radio Silence
Channel 16

MAYDAY
ALL STATIONS ALL STATIONS ALL STATIONS
THIS IS FALMOUTH COASTGUARD
TIME ONE ONE THREE FIVE GMT
YACHT JETTO
SEELONCE FEENEE
OUT

9

Urgency

When a very urgent message concerning the SAFETY OF A VESSEL or the SAFETY OF A PERSON needs to be transmitted, but the sending of a MAYDAY signal is not justified, the urgency signal PAN PAN is used. A call prefixed with the words PAN PAN has priority over all other calls except distress calls. The use of PAN PAN does not automatically impose radio silence but an immediate response should be expected.

PAN PAN may be used in the following situations:

A person has fallen overboard and has not been immediately recovered; someone has sustained a serious injury; a vessel is being carried into a dangerous position due to gear failure.

The Call:
1. PAN PAN three times.
2. ALL STATIONS three times (or the name of the station to which the PAN PAN is addressed).
3. The words: THIS IS.
4. The vessel's name or call sign three times.

The Message:
1. Position
2. The nature of the urgency and the assistance required
3. The word: OVER

If the message is addressed to ALL STATIONS, the transmitting station must cancel it by a similarly addressed message when she knows that further assistance is no longer required.

Urgency
Channel 16

The Call:
>   PAN PAN PAN PAN PAN PAN
>   ALL STATIONS ALL STATIONS ALL STATIONS

The Message:
>   THIS IS YACHT PLOVER YACHT PLOVER YACHT PLOVER
>   MY POSITION THREE MILES SOUTH OF SAINT CATHERINES
>   POINT ENGINE BROKEN DOWN AND DRIFTING INSHORE
>   TOW URGENTLY NEEDED
>   OVER

Cancelling the Message:
>   ALL STATIONS ALL STATIONS ALL STATIONS
>   THIS IS YACHT PLOVER YACHT PLOVER YACHT PLOVER
>   CANCEL MY PAN PAN I AM NOW UNDER TOW
>   NO FURTHER ASSISTANCE NEEDED
>   OUT

Medical Advice

If medical advice is required, the word MEDICO should be included in the call. Initial contact is made on Channel 16, but if a long conversation is likely to follow, the message may be passed on a working channel.

Urgency
Medical Advice

Initial call (Channel 16):
    PAN PAN PAN PAN PAN PAN MEDICO
    NORTH FORELAND RADIO NORTH FORELAND RADIO
      NORTH FORELAND RADIO
    THIS IS YACHT LAPWING YACHT LAPWING YACHT LAPWING
    I REQUIRE MEDICAL ADVICE I HAVE ALL CHANNELS
    OVER

        PAN PAN MEDICO
        YACHT LAPWING
        THIS IS NORTH FORELAND RADIO
        CHANGE TO CHANNEL TWENTY SIX
        OVER

Safety

The safety signal SECURITE (pronounced SAY-CURE-E-TAY) precedes an important navigational or meteorological warning. The initial call is made on Channel 16 but the message is transmitted on a working channel.

The Call (Channel 16):
1. The safety signal SECURITE three times.
2. ALL STATIONS three times.
3. The words THIS IS.
4. The identity of the station calling three times.
5. The initial announcement.

The Message (Working channel):
1. The safety signal SECURITE three times.
2. ALL STATIONS three times.
3. The words THIS IS.
4. The identity of the station calling three times.
5. The warning.
6. The word OUT.

A SECURITE message usually originates ashore but it can be broadcast by any station to report a navigational hazard.

Safety

The Call (Channel 16):
    SECURITE SECURITE SECURITE
    ALL STATIONS ALL STATIONS ALL STATIONS
    THIS IS NORTH FORELAND RADIO NORTH FORELAND
      RADIO NORTH FORELAND RADIO
    FOR REPETITION OF NAVIGATION WARNING BROADCAST
      LISTEN ON CHANNEL TWENTY SIX

The Message (Channel 26):
    SECURITE SECURITE SECURITE
    ALL STATIONS ALL STATIONS ALL STATIONS
    THIS IS NORTH FORELAND RADIO NORTH FORELAND
      RADIO NORTH FORELAND RADIO
    REPETITION OF NAVIGATION WARNING NUMBER THREE
      NINE ONE
    ENGLAND EAST COAST GREAT YARMOUTH APPROACHES
      EAST CROSS SAND BUOY REPORTED UNLIT
    THIS IS NORTH FORELAND RADIO
    LISTENING ON CHANNEL SIXTEEN AND ON DIRECT TRAFFIC
      CHANNEL CALLING CHANNEL TWENTY SIX CHANNEL
      FIVE AND CHANNEL SIXTY SIX
    OUT

(The warning part of the message is usually repeated.)

The Coastguard

Around the UK coast there are Maritime Rescue Co-ordination Centres manned by the Coastguard; some on a 24 hour basis. The principal duty of the Coastguard is to co-ordinate search and rescue operations and to maintain a continuous watch on Channel 16.

The Coastguard's normal working is on Channel 67 (though calling should be on Channel 16) and occasionally on Channel 73. Under special circumstances he may use Channel 06.

Each centre has access to at least two VHF radio direction finders (VHF/DF) to locate any vessel making a distress or urgency call. This is primarily for distress or urgency, but the Coastguard will pass a position to a vessel unsure of her location. For efficient operation the VHF/DF requires a transmission of about 10 seconds, so the Coastguard may request the vessel to press the transmit switch for a suitable period.

The Coastguard operate a Small Craft Safety Scheme. To register, complete Form CG66 part of which remains with the Coastguard and part with a responsible agent ashore. This form fully describes the vessel and her safety or radio equipment plus the name of the agent. Details of any passage planned are then left with the agent ashore, including time of departure, route and ETA. If the agent does not receive notification of the vessel's safe arrival at the expected time, he should get in touch with the Coastguard who will, if necessary, organise a search. Advance details of a long passage can also be telephoned to the Coastguard direct.

The example of safety traffic given here represents the procedure preferred by the Coastguard though the formal procedure omits the acknowledgement of the channel change by the calling station.

Small Boat Safety

Initial call (Channel 16):
    SOLENT COASTGUARD
    THIS IS YACHT PLOVER YACHT PLOVER
    SAFETY TRAFFIC
    OVER

        YACHT PLOVER
        THIS IS SOLENT COASTGUARD
        CHANNEL SIXTY SEVEN
        OVER

    SOLENT COASTGUARD
    THIS IS YACHT PLOVER
    CHANGING TO SIXTY SEVEN

Message (Channel 67):
        YACHT PLOVER
        THIS IS SOLENT COASTGUARD
        GO AHEAD PLEASE
        OVER

    SOLENT COASTGUARD
    THIS IS YACHT PLOVER
    I AM JUST PASSING CHRISTCHURCH LEDGE BUOY ON
      PASSAGE TO FALMOUTH ETA FRIDAY AFTERNOON TWENTY
      FIRST JUNE
    OVER

        YACHT PLOVER
        THIS IS SOLENT COASTGUARD
        ROGER I HAVE RECEIVED ALL THAT HAVE A
          PLEASANT TRIP
        OUT

Navigational Warnings and Weather Forecasts

Another service provided by the Coastguard is the broadcast of navigational and strong wind warnings. A weather forecast can also be obtained on request.

Yacht Safety Information Broadcasts

From time to time the Coastguard may wish to enlist the assistance of other vessels to locate a yacht which may, for instance, have been reported missing. The Yacht Safety Information (YSI) broadcast will be announced on Channel 16 and broadcast on Channel 67.

Channel Navigational Information Service

Dover Coastguard on Channel 10 and Gris Nez Traffic on Channel 11 jointly operate the Channel Navigation Information Service in the Straits of Dover. Broadcasts are made every half hour giving details of any navigational hazards. All shipping movements are monitored for compliance with the *International Regulations for Preventing Collisions at Sea*.

Yacht Safety Information Broadcast

Initial Call (Channel 16):

    ALL STATIONS ALL STATIONS ALL STATIONS

    THIS IS SOLENT COASTGUARD SOLENT COASTGUARD
       SOLENT COASTGUARD

    FOR A YACHT SAFETY INFORMATION BROADCAST LISTEN
       ON CHANNEL SIXTY SEVEN VHF

    THIS IS SOLENT COASTGUARD

Message (Channel 67):

    ALL STATIONS ALL STATIONS ALL STATIONS

    THIS IS SOLENT COASTGUARD SOLENT COASTGUARD
       SOLENT COASTGUARD

    YACHT SAFETY INFORMATION BROADCAST

    INFORMATION IS REQUESTED ON YACHT PELICAN

    LENGTH NINE METRES WHITE HULL AND SAILS

    NUMBER YANKEE SIX TWO THREE

    DEPARTED LYMINGTON ONE EIGHT ONE EIGHT ZERO ZERO
       GMT DESTINATION DARTMOUTH

    DATE TIME GROUP ONE NINE ZERO EIGHT ZERO ZERO GMT

    THIS IS SOLENT COASTGUARD

Coast Radio Station

A VHF radio telephone service, which includes 33 radio stations and extends 30 to 40 miles from the UK coastline, is maintained by British Telecom International.

British Coast Radio Stations should be contacted direct on a working channel. Details of channels available will be found in the *Admiralty List of Radio Signals Vol. 1, Admiralty List of Radio Services for Small Craft* and yachtsmen's almanacs.

The procedure for contacting a Coast Radio Station on a working channel is as follows:

1. Select the channel.
2. **Listen** first to see that the channel is free. If it is engaged, either speech or a series of pips will be heard.
3. Call the station. Your call should be at least 6 seconds as it takes that amount of time to activate the receiver which alerts the radio officer to your call.
4. When your call has activated the receiver you will hear the engaged signal so **wait** for the radio officer to respond.

Repeat the call if it is unanswered after three minutes.

Should the Coast Radio Station be dealing with several calls you may be asked to wait and given a number. You will then be called when it is your turn.

In a ship to shore communication the Coast Radio Station is the controlling station and any instructions given by it must be followed.

The yacht's call sign should be used when calling, in addition to or instead of the yacht's name. Some vessels' names are complex and difficult for the radio operator to record correctly, whereas call signs are much less ambiguous.

If the Coast Radio Station is very busy the radio officer may not hear the name or call sign of the vessel calling even though his receiver has latched on to the call, in which case he may say STATION CALLING NORTH FORELAND RADIO, GO AHEAD PLEASE. Some continental Coast Radio Stations (notably France) will not accept any calls except distress and urgency calls on Channel 16, and working channels must be used. When calling a French Coast Radio Station it is only necessary to hold the press-to-transmit switch for a period of at least 6 seconds and the radio officer will respond when he is free. The tone of the engaged signal from continental stations can vary.

Yacht Telephone Debit

Small craft based in the UK making a telephone call through a UK Coast Radio Station, provided that the call is to be connected to a telephone number in the UK, the Channel Islands or the Isle of Man, may have that call charged to their home or office telephone account by quoting their Accounting Authority Indicator Code as YTD followed by the number to which the call is to be charged.

GB14

If traffic is sent through a foreign Coast Radio Station, or if it does not fall within the category mentioned above, then the Accounting Authority Indicator Code issued with the Ship Licence (which for small craft is GB14) must be used.

Transferred Charges

Reversed charge calls can also be made where the recipient pays for the call. For this type of call an extra charge is made.

Making a Telephone Call
Channel 26

NORTH FORELAND RADIO
THIS IS YACHT PLOVER YACHT PLOVER
CALL SIGN MIKE ZULU ALFA BRAVO
ONE LINK CALL PLEASE
OVER

    YACHT PLOVER
    THIS IS NORTH FORELAND RADIO
    WHAT IS YOUR ACCOUNTING CODE AND WHAT
       NUMBER WOULD YOU LIKE
    OVER

NORTH FORELAND RADIO
THIS IS PLOVER
I WOULD LIKE A YTD CALL CHARGED TO ZERO EIGHT
   FOUR THREE TWO NINE TWO FIVE FIVE AND CONNECTED
   TO ZERO SIX ZERO TWO SEVEN ZERO SEVEN SEVEN
OVER

    YACHT PLOVER
    THIS IS NORTH FORELAND RADIO
    STAND BY

(pips will be heard)

    YACHT PLOVER THIS IS NORTH FORELAND RADIO
    YOU ARE CONNECTED GO AHEAD PLEASE. . .

Traffic Routeing

Before commencing a long passage, if any telephone calls are expected, details of the passage should be given to the nearest Coast Radio Station so that they can estimate your approximate position should it be necessary to contact you. This procedure is called Traffic Routeing shortened to TR.

By implication a vessel that has initiated a TR must listen out continuously on the calling channel (Channel 16).

Traffic Routeing
Channel 26

NORTH FORELAND RADIO
THIS IS YACHT LAPWING
MIKE BRAVO CHARLIE QUEBEC
I HAVE A TR FOR YOU
OVER

YACHT LAPWING
MIKE CHARLIE BRAVO QUEBEC
THIS IS NORTH FORELAND RADIO
GO AHEAD PLEASE
OVER

NORTH FORELAND RADIO
THIS IS YACHT LAPWING
I HAVE JUST LEFT RAMSGATE ON PASSAGE TO HAMBLE
  ETA HAMBLE WEDNESDAY MORNING SEVENTEENTH
  AUGUST
NOTHING MORE FOR YOU
OVER

YACHT LAPWING
THIS IS NORTH FORELAND
RECEIVED
OUT

Traffic Lists

At set times a TRAFFIC LIST is broadcast from Coast Radio Stations. This is a list of vessels for which there is traffic waiting. The traffic list is announced on Channel 16 and then broadcast on the primary working channel.

Traffic List

Announced on Channel 16:

    ALL SHIPS ALL SHIPS ALL SHIPS
    THIS IS NORTH FORELAND RADIO NORTH FORELAND
        RADIO NORTH FORELAND RADIO
    LISTEN FOR MY TRAFFIC LIST ON CHANNEL TWENTY-SIX

Broadcast on Channel 26:

    ALL SHIPS ALL SHIPS ALL SHIPS
    THIS IS NORTH FORELAND RADIO NORTH FORELAND
        RADIO NORTH FORELAND RADIO
    WE ARE HOLDING TRAFFIC FOR
    YACHT LAPWING MIKE BRAVO CHARLIE QUEBEC AND
    YACHT PLOVER MIKE ZULU ALFA BRAVO
    THIS IS NORTH FORELAND RADIO
    LISTENING OUT ON CHANNEL SIXTEEN AND ON DIRECT
        TRAFFIC CHANNEL CALLING CHANNEL TWENTY SIX
        CHANNEL FIVE AND CHANNEL SIXTY SIX
    OUT

Closing Down Radio Watch

Upon arrival at her destination the vessel must inform the local Coast Radio Station that she is CLOSING DOWN RADIO WATCH. The Coast Radio Station will then pass on any outstanding traffic.

Closing Down Radio Watch
Channel 28

NITON RADIO
THIS IS YACHT LAPWING YACHT LAPWING
CALL SIGN MIKE BRAVO CHARLIE QUEBEC
OVER

    YACHT LAPWING
    THIS IS NITON RADIO
    OVER

NITON RADIO
THIS IS YACHT LAPWING
NOW BERTHED AT HAMBLE
CLOSING DOWN RADIO WATCH
OVER

    YACHT LAPWING
    THIS IS NITON RADIO
    ACKNOWLEDGED
    NOTHING FOR YOU
    OUT

Contacting A Vessel At Sea

If a person ashore wishes to contact a vessel at sea, he should dial 100 and ask for SHIP'S TELEPHONE SERVICE giving the name of the Coast Radio Station thought to be nearest to the vessel's position. The Coast Radio Station will ask for the vessel's call sign, her approximate position and her Selcall number if known.

An attempt will then be made to contact the vessel in one of the following ways:

1. Directly calling her on Channel 16.
2. Activating her Selcall.
3. Including her name in the next traffic list.

Urgent or Personal Messages

For vessels who have receivers only, there is a broadcast service immediately after the morning and evening weather bulletins for passing urgent or personal messages to them. To send such a message contact the Coast Radio Station nearest to the vessel's position and ask for YACHTING RADIO MESSAGES.

Weather Forecasts

These are broadcast twice daily. They are announced first on Channel 16 and then broadcast on the primary working channel.

Gale Warnings
These are broadcast in the same manner as weather forecasts, immediately on receipt and then at set times thereafter.

Port Operation

Port Radio Stations are normally called direct on a working channel. Channels 12 and 14 are the common Port Operation channels. A full list of channels used by specific ports will be found in *Admiralty List of Radio Signals Vol. 6*, *Admiralty List Radio Services for Small Craft*, and yachtsmen's almanacs.

A small craft entering a port area can learn about shipping movements and navigational warnings by monitoring the local port operations channel. If a yacht is likely to require any port services (like passing through a lock) she is encouraged to call the Port Radio Station giving details of her requirements and estimated times of arrival at key points.

Port Operation
Channel 12

ALL SHIPS THIS IS GRAVESEND RADIO WITH THE RIVER
   BROADCAST FOR TEN HUNDRED
NAVIGATIONAL INFORMATION
SURVEY OPERATIONS TAKING PLACE IN THE PRINCES
   CHANNEL THE TANKER TRAFFIC WARNING LIGHTS ARE
   BEING DISPLAYED FOR THE LA FALDA BERTHING NOW AT
   BRAVO JETTY SHELLHAVEN
TIDAL INFORMATION
TIDE AT WALTON ZERO POINT SIX METRES MARGATE ZERO
   POINT SIX METRES SOUTHEND ZERO POINT SIX METRES
   AND TILBURY ZERO POINT EIGHT METRES
ALL HEIGHTS ARE ABOVE DATUM
END OF BROADCAST
GRAVESEND
OUT

Channel M

Channel M is a private channel used to enable yachts to contact marinas and for race control by yacht clubs. It may only be used for business concerning berthing and must not be used to pass messages ashore which should be done through the Coast Radio Station.

Channel M

HAMBLE YACHT HARBOUR
THIS IS YACHT LAPWING
HAVE YOU A BERTH AVAILABLE PLEASE
OVER

> YACHT LAPWING
> THIS IS HAMBLE YACHT HARBOUR
> WHAT IS YOUR LENGTH AND DRAUGHT
> HOW MANY NIGHTS ARE YOU STAYING
> OVER

HAMBLE YACHT HARBOUR
THIS IS YACHT LAPWING
LENGTH TEN POINT NINE METRES
DRAUGHT ONE POINT NINE METRES
ONE NIGHT ONLY
OVER

> YACHT LAPWING
> THIS IS HAMBLE YACHT HARBOUR
> STAND BY. . .

> YACHT LAPWING THIS IS HAMBLE YACHT HARBOUR
> TAKE BERTH CHARLIE FOUR SIX UPRIVER SIDE PORT
>   SIDE TO NEXT TO MOTOR CRUISER SHAMBLES
> OVER

HAMBLE YACHT HARBOUR
THIS IS YACHT LAPWING
CONFIRM BERTH CHARLIE FOUR SIX PORT SIDE TO ALONG-
    SIDE SHAMBLES
BE WITH YOU IN TWENTY MINUTES
OUT

Intership (Ship to Ship)

The initial call to another vessel can be made either on Channel 16 and then transferred to an intership channel or (by prior arrangement) directly on an intership channel. Once communication is established on the intership channel, the procedure may be less formal than for other traffic; but the transmitting station must always give her identity.

Do not use an intership channel for gossip. Remember other vessels may be waiting to make a call and, of course, everyone within range can overhear you.

Use low power if possible.

In intership communications the vessel being called is the controlling vessel.

Note: In formal communications each station completes her last transmission with the word OUT.

Intership

Channel 16:
YACHT SKYLARK
THIS IS YACHT NIGHTINGALE
OVER

> YACHT NIGHTINGALE
> THIS IS YACHT SKYLARK
> CHANNEL SEVENTY TWO
> OVER

YACHT SKYLARK
THIS IS YACHT NIGHTINGALE
CHANGING TO SEVENTY TWO

Channel 72:
> YACHT NIGHTINGALE
> THIS IS YACHT SKYLARK
> GO AHEAD
> OVER

YACHT SKYLARK
THIS IS YACHT NIGHTINGALE
WHERE ARE YOU NOW
OVER

> YACHT NIGHTINGALE
> THIS IS YACHT SKYLARK
> WE ARE ABOUT TWO MILES EAST OF LULWORTH
>   COVE
> WE SHOULD BE THERE IN HALF AN HOUR
> OVER

THIS IS YACHT NIGHTINGALE
GOOD WE SHOULD BE THERE AT ABOUT THE SAME TIME
OVER

continued overleaf

THIS IS YACHT SKYLARK
FINE THEN SEE YOU THERE
OUT

THIS IS YACHT NIGHTINGALE
OUT

Garbled Calls

If a garbled call is received and the name of the station called is not heard, no answer should be made until the call has been repeated and the name of the station called identified.

If a station identified in a call cannot make out the identity of the calling station she should request a repeat of the call by using the words STATION CALLING . . . SAY AGAIN.

Contacting an Unidentified Vessel

If it is necessary to contact another vessel visible but too far distant to identify, then that vessel may be called by giving her position, usually in relation to a prominent landmark. The message is addressed to ALL SHIPS:

ALL SHIPS THIS IS YACHT BLACKBIRD
VESSEL TWO MILES SOUTH OF NAB TOWER. . .

Radio Check

The correct operation of a VHF radio may be checked by calling another vessel, a Coast Radio Station (preferably on a working channel) or the Coastguard, and requesting a RADIO CHECK. This should not last longer than 10 seconds.

Radio Telegrams

Radio telegrams may be sent using the same procedure as for link calls. (See page 23.)

VHF Radio Lighthouses

VHF Radio lighthouses are used for navigation in specific areas, normally operating on Channel 88. A series of pips are transmitted by the radio lighthouse from which a bearing can be obtained by counting until the pips fade. Details of operation are contained in *Admiralty List of Radio Signals*, *Admiralty List of Radio Signals for Small Craft* and yachtsmen's almanacs.

VHF RADIO EQUIPMENT

The standard VHF radio set fitted in a yacht will have 55 international channels, high and low power output, a Dual Watch facility and a masthead aerial. With modern electronics it is uneconomical to have anything less than the standard set. The difference in price between sets can give an indication of their robustness and reliability.

Range

VHF communication is line of sight, which means that the operating range is constrained by the curvature of the earth. The height of the aerial above sea level is, therefore, the most important factor affecting range. With a standard set, a yachtsman might expect to communicate with a shore station at a distance away up to 40 miles and, with another yacht, up to 20 miles.

At these ranges the High Power output is selected. High Power corresponds to a transmitted output power of 25 watts, which is the maximum permitted for this type of set. For ranges of less than 2 miles, the Low Power output (1 watt) should be used so as not to cause interference with other vessels further away.

Capture Effects

A VHF radio set in the receiving mode (this is the normal state when the press-to-transmit switch is not pressed) will lock on to or *capture* the strongest signal it receives on the selected channel. This means that a conversation already in progress can be blotted out by another station transmitting inconsiderately. Therefore, it is essential to **wait and listen** before making a transmission; particularly to a Coast Radio Station who may already be communicating with a distant station which itself may not be audible. (See Fig. 1 below.)

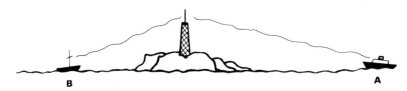

Fig. 1. Vessel A is transmitting to the Coast Radio Station. Vessel B cannot hear vessel A, and also transmits a message to the Coast Radio Station. Because vessel B is nearer, her transmission interrupts the transmission from vessel A.

Simplex or Duplex

Some VHF radio channels are allocated two separate frequencies and others only one. A *duplex* channel has two frequencies, one of which is used for transmission and the other for reception. However, each of these frequencies needs a separate aerial which is impractical on a small craft. For such craft, when the press-to-transmit switch is depressed, the set will transmit on one frequency and when it is released the set will receive on another. This is known as *semi-duplex* operation and it enables a craft with a single aerial to communicate with a shore station with two separate aerials. For a *simplex* channel with only one operating frequency both transmission and reception is on that frequency.

Duplex channels are used in communications with Coast Radio Stations and certain Port Radio Stations but not for intership working.

Controls (See Plate 1)

Squelch

Every VHF radio set is fitted with a control marked *squelch*. The squelch control sets the threshold of the received signal relative to the receiver noise. In practice it is adjusted until the receiver noise is just suppressed. If the transmitting station is far away it may not be possible to eliminate all receiver noise when trying to pick up a weak signal.

Plate 1. A radiotelephone. This is a Seavoice RT 550 made by Seafarer International Ltd. (Photo reproduced by courtesy of Seafarer Navigation International Ltd.)

Microphone Transmit Switch (Press-to-Transmit Switch)

To make a transmission, the press-to-transmit switch on the microphone or telephone handset is depressed. With the switch in this position, anything spoken into the microphone will be broadcast. Whilst transmitting, the set cannot receive any other radio transmission nor can any other station within range use that channel. To receive, the press-to-transmit switch must be released. Should this switch become accidentally jammed in the transmitting position, the overall effect is disastrous as no other station can use that channel.

Dual Watch

The control for Dual Watch normally has three positions. Position one: OFF. Position two: CHANNEL 16. Position three: DUAL WATCH. The set operates normally with the switch in the OFF position. When Channel 16 is selected, the set is switched directly to Channel 16 by-passing the channel selector. When switched to DUAL WATCH the selected channel is monitored but for a very short period (a fifth of a second) at intervals (of approximately one second) Channel 16 is monitored. If a received signal is present on Channel 16, the set will lock on to that channel until the signal ceases, whereupon it will revert to the selected channel. Thus the selected channel can be monitored but it is overridden by any signals received on Channel 16.

On some radio sets DUAL WATCH must be switched off before transmitting on the selected channel.

Selcall

An additional attachment for the VHF radio is the selective calling feature known as *Selcall*. A vessel fitted with this feature has, in addition to her call sign, a unique Selcall number. The Coast Radio Station can call that vessel by transmitting a very brief signal containing a coded version of this number. The Selcall will decode the number and if it corresponds with that allocated to the vessel an alarm buzzer and light are activated. The vessel can then call the Coast Radio Station in the normal manner. For navigational warnings or meteorological information the CRS can transmit a coded signal which will activate the Selcall on all ships within range.

Channels

A VHF radio operates on channels 01 to 28, and 60 to 88. The channels are divided into 3 groups: (a) public correspondence; (b) port operation; (c) intership working. Some channels have a dual purpose but Coast and Port Radio stations operate on different frequencies. Appendix III gives list of channels.

Channel 16

Channel 16 is for distress, safety and calling only. For safety and calling its function is for the direction of users to a working channel. Distress, followed by Urgency, traffic has complete priority on this channel. All transmissions other than for distress or urgency traffic must not exceed one minute.

Channels 67, 73, 06, 00

In UK waters Channel 67 is used by the Coastguard for matters concerned with small boat safety. He may also use an alternative, Channel 73, and in special circumstances Channel 06. Additionally he has the exclusive use of private Channel 00. This channel can only be fitted to a VHF set with special permission from the Home Office if the operator is an Auxiliary Coastguard.

Channel 70

Selective call, distress and safety.

Channel 76

Direct printing telegraphy, distress and safety.

Channel 88

In certain areas, Channel 88 is used as a navigational aid in conjunction with VHF Radio Lighthouses.

Private Channels

On some sets up to five additional private channels can be selected. One of these is Channel 37 which is called Channel M. This is for use, in UK waters, by marinas for berthing operations and also by yacht clubs for race organisation. It is not intended to be used as an intership channel, nor is it permitted to use it to pass a message intended for a party ashore.

Portable Transceivers

Some portable VHF radios (transceivers) have only a limited number of channels. In these cases Channels 16 and 06 are mandatory.

Additional Loudspeaker

Proper use of VHF radio on small craft implies that the radio should be monitored constantly (normally on Channel 16) whilst at sea. It is useful, therefore, to have an additional weatherproof loudspeaker in the vicinity of the helming position, which can be switched on when the radio position, normally near the chart table, is unmanned.

Licences

For a vessel fitted with a VHF radiotelephone a Ship Licence is required which authorises the establishment and use of a sending and receiving station.

If a receiver only is installed for receiving messages from Coast Radio Stations (and certain other stations) a Ship (Receiving Only) Licence is needed.

For a radio used **only** in emergency, a Ship (Emergency Only) Licence is all that is necessary.

A ship will be issued with a Callsign, Accounting Authority Indicator Code (normally GB14 for small craft) and a Selcall number (if appropriate) when the Ship Licence is issued.

Operator's Certificate of Competence

Except in distress, an Operator's Certificate of Competence is required for an operator to make a transmission. Another person may operate the set but only when directly supervised by a qualified operator. For VHF radio operating only, this certificate is known as the Restricted Certificate of Competence in Radio Telephony VHF Only.

Emergency Position Indicating Radio Beacon (EPIRB) Merchant Shipping Notice M982 (See Appendix IV)

An EPIRB is a small transmitter used only in distress. It transmits an alarm signal on frequencies used by aircraft (121.5 MHz and 243 MHz), and also on the medium wave distress frequency (2182 kHz). Their purpose is to determine the position of survivors during search and rescue operations.

QUESTION PAPER

1. What is the distress signal?
2. You are in a yacht named *Sparrow*. Your position is 10 miles south of Start Point. You have struck an unidentified floating object and are sinking. There are 7 people on board. Send the appropriate message.
3. You are the controlling station during a distress, and wish to impose radio silence. What are the words you would use to do this?
4. You hear an unanswered distress call but are too far away to render assistance and so you re-broadcast the message. How will you indicate that you are not yourself in distress?
5. What do the following words mean when used in connection with distress traffic?
   a) PRUDONCE
   b) SEELONCE FEENEE
6. Would it be correct to use the distress signal if you lost a person overboard and could not locate him?
7. What is the word used to request medical advice?
8. Upon which channel will a SECURITE message be transmitted?
9. Which channel should you use when calling the Coastguard?
10. Before making a call, what should you do?
11. List the intership channels which are used solely for this purpose.
12. Is it correct to call a Coast Radio Station on a working channel?
13. a) Are you allowed to transmit short messages on Channel 16?
    b) What is the maximum time allowed for a transmission on Channel 16 (apart from distress, urgency and safety traffic)?
14. How long should a test transmission last?

15. If you had not been keeping a radio watch, how could you find out if there were any messages for you?
16. Upon which channel should you call another ship?
17. Is it permissible to transmit a message without using your station's identity?
18. Can Channel M be used for an intership channel?
19. For what is Channel 06 used?
20. For what are Channels 12 and 14 used?
21. Your selective calling device is activated by a multitone signal on Channel 16. Detail the procedure so that you can be put in contact with the caller.
22. In a position 15 miles offshore you sight to seaward a red rocket flare. What action will you take?
23. You are approaching Dover Harbour and you wish to know whether the entrance is clear for you to enter. How do you find this out?
24. You are about to cross the Traffic Separation Scheme south of Varne Light Vessel, south east of Dover. What should you do?
25. Proceeding up the river Thames, you estimate that you will arrive at the Thames Barrier in about 30 minutes. What should you do?

Answers are on page 80.

Appendix I   Regulations

A complete set of regulations is printed in the Ship Licence; some of the important ones are mentioned below:

1. Transmissions which are not authorised by the licensee (usually the person in charge) are not allowed.
2. The radio must be operated either by a person holding the Operators Certificate of Competence who has been given authority to operate by the Secretary of State; OR by a person under the direct control of the holder of such a certificate.
3. The Ship Station's identity must be used in all transmissions.
4. Channels must only be used for their designated purpose.
5. All ship-to-shore messages must be transmitted through a Coast Radio Station.
6. Superfluous correspondence must be avoided.
7. Profane and obscene language must not be used.
8. Transmissions must not be made in harbour except through a Coast Radio Station.
9. The contents of any message accidentally overheard must not be disclosed.
10. False distress signals or misleading messages must not be transmitted.
11. It is not allowed to transmit music.
12. Messages which do not require a reply must not be broadcast (the exception being an ALL STATIONS broadcast).

Appendix II Documents to be Carried on Board

1. The Ship Licence.
2. Copy of Section II of the Post Office (Protection) Act 1884.
3. Operators certificate.
4. The radiotelephone log. (See *Note*, below.)
5. A list of Coast Radio Stations with which communications are likely to be conducted.
6. Post Office Handbook for Radio Operators.
7. Complete file of current *Notices to Ship Wireless Stations*.

Note. The regulations require that every vessel fitted with a radio telephone should keep a radiotelephone log which provides a record of messages transmitted and received. Each entry should include: the Greenwich Mean Time of the message; the identity of the station called; the identity of the calling station; and the context of the message.

Appendix III   VHF Channels

Channel	Public Correspondence	Port Operations and Ship Movement	Intership
01	*	*	
02	*	*	
03	*	*	
04	*	*	
05	*	*	
06			*
07	*	*	
08			*
09		*	*
10		*	*
11		*	
12		*	
13		*	*
14		*	
15		*	*
16	D I S T R E S S S A F E T Y C A L L I N G		
17		*	*
18		*	
19		*	
20		*	

Channel	Public Correspondence	Port Operations and Ship Movement	Intership
21		*	
22		*	
23	*		
24	*		
25	*		
26	*		
27	*		
28	*		
60	*	*	
61	*	*	
62	*	*	
63	*	*	
64	*	*	
65	*	*	
66	*	*	
67	Small boat safety channel		
68		*	
69		*	*
70	Digital selective calling – distress & safety		
71		*	
72			*
73		*	*

Channel	Public Correspondence	Port Operations and Ship Movement	Intership
74		*	
76	Direct printing telegraphy – distress & safety		
77			*
78	*	*	
79		*	
80		*	
81	*	*	
82	*	*	
83	*		
84	*	*	
85	*		
86	*		
87	*		
88	*		

Appendix IV Merchant Shipping Notices

DEPARTMENT OF TRADE   MERCHANT SHIPPING NOTICE NO. **M.1026**

PROPER USE OF VHF CHANNELS AT SEA

Notice to Owners, Masters and Officers of Merchant Ships, Owners and Skippers of Fishing Vessels and Owners of Yachts

This Notice supersedes Notice No. M 814

1. The International Maritime Organisation (IMO, formerly IMCO) has noted with concern the widespread misuse of VHF channels at sea. This misuse is causing serious interference to essential communications and is a potential danger to safety at sea. IMO has asked Member Governments to ensure that VHF channels are used correctly and that, in particular, the following transmissions are avoided:

   a. Ship-to-ship communications on Channel 16 except for distress communications and for calling to establish other communications which should then be conducted on a suitable working channel;

   b. Ship-to-ship communications on the channels allocated to port operations, ship movement services and reporting systems, other than those for the movement and safety of shipping;

   c. Superfluous signals and correspondence;

   d. Signals without station identification.

2. The Appendix to this Notice consists of notes on guidance on the use of VHF at sea which IMO has asked Member Governments to bring to the attention of all concerned.

3. Masters and Skippers are urged to ensure that VHF channels are used in accordance with the Appendix to this Notice.

4. The introduction of reduced channel spacing in the international maritime mobile VHF frequency band has made it possible to allocate more frequencies for ship-to-ship communications and of these channels 6, 8, 70, 72, and 77 are now available exclusively for this purpose. Owners are urged to fit as many of these channels as possible and Masters and Skippers are urged to ensure that all ship-to-ship working in UK waters is confined to these channels, selecting that most appropriate in the light of local conditions at the time.

Department of Trade
Marine Division
London WC1V 6LP
July 1982

GUIDANCE ON THE USE OF VHF AT SEA

1. VHF communication technique

1.1 *Preparation*
Before transmitting, think about the subjects which have to be communicated and, if necessary, prepare written notes to avoid unnecessary interruptions and ensure that no valuable time is wasted on a busy channel.

1.2 *Listening*
Listen before commencing to transmit to make certain that the channel is not already in use. This will avoid unnecessary and irritating interference.

1.3 *Discipline*
VHF equipment should be used correctly and in accordance with the Radio Regulations. The following in particular should be avoided:
.1 calling on Channel 16 for purposes other than distress, urgency and very brief safety communications when another calling channel is available;
.2 communications not related to safety and navigation on port operation channels;
.3 non-essential transmissions, e.g. needless and superfluous signals and correspondence;
.4 transmitting without correct identification;
.5 occupation of one particular channel under poor conditions;
.6 use of offensive language.

1.4 *Repetition*
Repetition of words and phrases should be avoided unless specifically requested by the receiving station.

1.5 *Power reduction*
When possible, the lowest transmitter power necessary for satisfactory communication should be used.

1.6 *Communications with shore stations*

1.6.1 Instructions given on communication matters by shore stations should be obeyed.

1.6.2 Communications should be carried out on the channel indicated by the shore station. When a change of channel is requested, this should be acknowledged by the ship.

1.6.3 On receiving instructions from a shore station to stop transmitting, no further communications should be made until otherwise notified (the shore station may be receiving distress or safety messages and any other transmissions could cause interference).

1.7 *Communications with other ships*

1.7.1 During ship-to-ship communications the ship called should indicate the channel on which further transmissions should take place. The calling ship should acknowledge acceptance before changing channel.

1.7.2 The listening procedure outlined in paragraph 1.2 sshould be followed before communications are commenced on the chosen channel.

1.8 *Distress communications*

1.8.1 Distress calls/messages have absolute priority over all other communications. When hearing them all other transmissions should cease and a listening watch should be kept.

1.8.2 Any distress call/message should be recorded in the ship's log and passed to the master.

1.8.3 On receipt of a distress message, if in the vicinity, immediately acknowledge receipt. If not in the vicinity, allow a short interval of time to elapse before acknowledging receipt of the message in order to permit ships nearer to the distress to do so.

1.9 *Calling*

1.9.1 Whenever possible, a working frequency should be used. If a working frequency is not available, Channel 16 may be used, provided it is not occupied by a distress call/message.

1.9.2 In case of difficulty to establish contact with a ship or shore station, allow adequate time before repeating the call. Do not occupy the channel unnecessarily and try another channel.

1.10 *Changing channels*
If communications on a channel are unsatisfactory, indicate change of channel and await confirmation.

1.11 *Spelling*
If spelling becomes necessary (e.g. descriptive names, call signs, words which could be misunderstood) use the spelling table contained in the International Code of Signals and the Radio Regulations.

1.12 *Addressing*

The words "I" and "You" should be used prudently. Indicate to whom they refer.

Example:
Seaship, this is Port Radar, Port Radar, do you have a pilot?
Port Radar, this is Seaship, I do have a pilot.

1.13 *Watchkeeping*

1.13.1 Ships fitted only with VHF equipment should maintain watch on Channel 16 when at sea.

1.13.2 Other ships should, where practicable, keep watch on Channel 16 when within the service area of a shore station capable of operating on that channel.

1.13.3 In certain cases Governments may require ships to keep a watch on other channels.

2. VHF communication procedure

2.1 *Calling*

When calling a shore station or another ship, say the name of that shore station or ship once (twice if considered necessary in heavy radio traffic conditions) followed by the phrase THIS IS and the ship's name twice, indicating the channel in use.

Example:
Port City, this is Seastar, Seastar, on Channel 14.

2.2 *Exchange of messages*

2.2.1 When communicating with a ship whose name is unknown but whose position is known, that position may be used. In this case the call is addressed to all ships.

Example:
Hello all ships, this is Pastoria, Pastoria. Ship approaching number four buoy, I am passing Belinda Bank Light.

2.2.2 Where a message is received and only acknowledgement of receipt is needed, say "received". Where a message is received and acknowledgement of the correct message is required, say "received, understood", and repeat message if considered necessary.

Example:
Message: Your berth will be clear at 0830 hours.
Reply: Received, understood. Berth clear at 0830 hours.

2.2.3 During exchange of messages, a ship should invite a reply by saying "over".

2.2.4   Where appropriate, the following message should be sent:
"Please use/I will use, the Standard Marine Navigational Vocabulary".

When language difficulties exist which cannot be resolved by the use of the Vocabulary, the International Code of Signals should be used.

In this case the word "INTERCO" should precede the groups of the International Code of Signals.

Example:
"Please use/I will use the International Code of Signals".

2.2.5   Where message contains instructions or advice, the substance should be repeated.

Example:
Message: Advise you pass astern of me.
Reply: I will pass astern of you.

2.2.6   If a message is not properly received, ask for it to be repeated by saying "Say again".

2.2.7   If a message is received but not understood, say "Message not understood".

2.2.8   If it is necessary to change to a different channel say "Change to channel . . ." and wait for acknowledgement before carrying out the change.

2.2.9   The end of a communication is indicated by the word "out".

3   Standard messages

3.1   Since most ship-to-shore communications are exchanges of information, it is advisable to use standard messages which will reduce transmission time.

3.2   Commonly used standard messages are given in the following Table and examples. Further samples of standard messages are given in the Standard Marine Navigational Vocabulary, which should be used whenever possible.

STANDARD MARINE NAVIGATIONAL VOCABULARY

Notice to Owners, Masters, Officers and Seamen of Merchant Ships, Yachts and other Sea-going Vessels. Owners, Skippers and Crews of Fishing Vessels. Pilots. Operators of Vessel Traffic Systems. Nautical Colleges. Coast Radio Stations.

This Notice supersedes Notice No. M.1018

1.   The Standard Marine Navigational Vocabulary developed by the International Maritime Organisation (IMO) has recently been extensively revised and the definitive version is annexed to this Notice. This will come into use on 1 January 1987.

2.   The main part of the Vocabulary has been divided into four parts, Part I contains General Instructions, Part II is a Glossary of Terms, Part III deals with communications external to the ship and Part IV with on-board communications covering pilot related matters.

3.   All those to whom the Notice is addressed are recommended to use the Vocabulary to minimise the possibility of misunderstanding vital information. In this context attention is drawn to the use of Message Markers as set out in Part I of this document.

Department of Transport
Marine Directorate
London WC1V 6LP
January 1987

INTRODUCTION

This vocabulary has been compiled:

- to assist in the greater safety of navigation and of the conduct of ships.
- to standardize the language used in communication for navigation at sea, in port-approaches, in waterways and harbours.

These phrases are not intended to supplant or contradict the International Regulations for Preventing Collisions at Sea or special local rules or recommendations made by IMO concerning ships' routeing. Neither are they intended to supersede the International Code of Signals nor to supplant normal radiotelephone practice as set out in the ITU Regulations.

It is not intended that use of the vocabulary shall be mandatory, but rather that through constant repetition in ships and in training establishments ashore, the phrases and terms used will become those normally accepted and commonplace among seamen. Use of the contents of the vocabulary should be made as often as possible in preference to other wording of similar meaning.

In this way it is intended to become an acceptable "language", using the English tongue, for the interchange of intelligence between individuals of all maritime nations on the many and varied occasions when precise meanings and translations are in doubt, increasingly evident under modern conditions at sea.

The typographical conventions used throughout most of this vocabulary are as follows:

() brackets indicate that the part of the message enclosed within the brackets may be added where it is relevant.

/ oblique stroke indicates that the items on either side of the stroke are alternatives.

. . . dots indicate that the relevant information is to be filled in where the dots occur.

STANDARD MARINE NAVIGATIONAL VOCABULARY

When spelling is necessary, only the letter spelling table contained in the international code of signals, chapter X, and in the radio regulations should be used.

PART 1

GENERAL

1 **Procedure/message markers**

When it is necessary to indicate that phrases in this vocabulary are to be used, the following messages may be sent:

"Please use the Standard Marine Navigational Vocabulary."
"I will use the Standard Marine Navigational Vocabulary."

If necessary, external communication messages may be preceded by the following message markers:

QUESTION	indicates that the following message is of interrogative character
ANSWER	indicates that the following message is the reply to a previous question
REQUEST	indicates that the contents of the following message are asking for action from others with respect to the ship
INFORMATION	indicates that the following message is restricted to observed facts
INTENTION	indicates that the following message informs others about immediate navigational actions intended to be taken
WARNING	indicates that the following message informs other traffic participants about dangers
ADVICE	indicates that the following message implies the intention of the sender to influence the recipient(s) by a recommendation
INSTRUCTION	indicates that the following message implies the intention of the sender to influence the recipient(s) by a regulation.

2 Standard verbs

Where possible, sentences should be introduced by one of the following verb forms:

IMPERATIVE
Always to be used when mandatory orders are being given

You must	Do not	Must I?

INDICATIVE	NEGATIVE	INTERROGATIVE
I require	I do not require	Do I require?
I am	I am not	Am I?
You are	You are not	Are you?
I have	I do not have	Do you have?
I can	I cannot	Can I? _ is it
		Can you? ‾ possible?
I wish to	I do not wish to	Do you wish to?
I will – *future*	I will not – *future*	
You may	You need not	May I? – *permission*
Advise	Advise not	
There is	There is not	Is there?
		What is/are?
		Where is/are?
		When is/are?

Note: See section 1 – Message markers.

3 Responses

Where the answer to a question is in the affirmative, say:
"yes . . ." – followed by the appropriate phrase in full.
Where the answer to a question is in the negative, say:
"no . . ." – followed by the appropriate phrase in full.
Where the information is not immediately available but soon will be, say:
"Stand by".

Where the information cannot be obtained, say:
"No information".
Where a message is not properly heard, say:
"Say again".
Whcre a message is not understood, say:
"Message not understood".

4 **Distress/urgency/safety messages**

MAYDAY (repeated three times)	is to be used to announce a distress message
PAN PAN (repeated three times)	is to be used to announce an urgency message
SECURITE (repeated three times)	is to be used to announce a safety message

5 **Miscellaneous phrases**
5.1 What is your name (and call sign)?
5.2 How do you read me?
5.3 I read you . . .   with signal strength . . .
    (bad/1)   (1/barely perceptible)
    (poor/2)   (2/weak)
    (fair/3)   (3/fairly good)
    (good/4)   (4/good)
    (excellent/5) (5/very good).
5.4 Stand by on channel . . .
5.5 Change to channel . . .
5.6 I cannot read you.
(Pass your message through vessel . . .).
(Advise try channel . . .).
5.7 I cannot understand you.
Please use the . . .
    (Standard Marine Navigational Vocabulary).
    (International Code of Signals).
5.8 I am passing a message for vessel . . .
5.9 Correction . . .

5.10 I am ready to receive your message.

5.11 I am not ready to receive your message.

5.12 I do not have channel . . . Please use channel . . .

6 Repetition

If any parts of the message are considered sufficiently important to need safeguarding, use the word "repeat".

> *Examples:* "You will load 163 repeat 163 tons bunkers."
> "Do not repeat not overtake."

7 Position

When latitude and longitude are used, these shall be expressed in degrees and minutes (and decimals of a minute if necessary), north or south of the Equator and east or west of Greenwich.

When the position is related to a mark, the mark shall be a well-defined charted object. The bearing shall be in the 360 degree notation from true north and shall be that of the position FROM the mark.

> *Examples:* "There are salvage operations in position 15 degrees 34 minutes north 61 degrees 29 minutes west."
> "Your position is 137 degrees from Barr Head lighthouse distance two decimal four miles."

8 Courses

Always to be expressed in 360 degree notation from north (true north unless otherwise stated). Whether this is to TO or FROM a mark can be stated.

9 Bearings

The bearing of the mark or vessel concerned, is the bearing in the 360 degree notation from north (true north unless otherwise stated), except in the case of relative bearings. Bearings may be either FROM the mark or FROM the vessel.

> *Examples:* "The pilot boat is bearing 215° from you."
> "Your bearing is 127° from the signal station."

Note: Vessels reporting their position should always quote their bearing FROM the mark, as described in paragraph 7.

Relative bearings

Relative bearings can be expressed in degrees relative to the vessel's head or bow. More frequently this is in relation to the port or starboard bow.

Example: "The buoy is 030° on your port bow."

Relative D/F bearings are more commonly expressed in the 360 degree notation.

10 Distances

Preferably to be expressed in nautical miles or cables (tenths of a mile) otherwise in kilometres or metres, the unit always to be stated.

11 Speed

To be expressed in knots:

(a) without further notation meaning speed through the water; or

(b) "ground speed" meaning speed over the ground.

12 Numbers

Numbers are to be spoken:

"One-five-zero" for 150.

"Two point five" for 2.5.

13 Geographical names

Place names should be those on the chart or Sailing Directions in use. Should these not be understood, latitude and longitude should be given.

14 Time

Times should be expressed in the 24 hour notation indicating whether UTC, zone time or local shore time is being used.

Note: In cases not covered by the above phraseology normal radio-telephone practice will prevail.

PART II

GLOSSARY

1 General

Air draught	Height of highest point of vessel's structure above waterline, e.g. radar, funnel, cranes, masthead.
Anchor position	Place where a specific vessel is anchored or is to anchor.
Calling-in-point (C.I.P.)	(see way point).
"Correction"	An error has been made in this transmission, the corrected version is . . .
Dragging (of anchor)	An anchor moving over the sea bottom involuntarily because it is no longer preventing the movement of the vessel.
Dredging anchor	Vessel moving, under control, with anchor moving along the sea bottom.
Draught	Depth from waterline to vessel's bottom, maximum/deepest unless otherwise specified.
Established	Brought into service, placed in position.
ETA	Estimated time of arrival.
ETD	Estimated time of departure.
Fairway	Navigable part of waterway.
Fairway speed	Mandatory speed in a fairway.
Foul (anchor)	Anchor has its own cable twisted around it or has fouled an obstruction.
Foul (propeller)	A line, wire, net, etc. is wound round the propeller.
Hampered vessel	A vessel restricted in her ability to manoeuvre by the nature of her work.
Icing	Formation of ice on vessels.
Inoperative	Not functioning.
Mark	General term for a navigational mark, e.g. buoy, structure or topographical feature which may be used to fix a vessel's position.
Offshore installation	Any offshore structure (e.g. a drilling rig, production platform, etc.) which may present a hazard to navigation.
Receiving point	A mark or place at which a vessel comes under obligatory entry, transit, or escort procedure (such as for port entry, canal transit or ice-breaker escort).
Reporting point	(see way point).
Vessel crossing	A vessel proceeding across a fairway/traffic lane/route.
Vessel inward	A vessel which is proceeding from sea to harbour or dock.
Vessel leaving	A vessel which is in the process of leaving a berth or anchorage. (When she has entered the navigable

	fairway she will be referred to as an outward, inward, crossing or turning vessel.)
Vessel outward	A vessel which is proceeding from harbour or anchorage to seawards.
Vessel turning	A vessel making LARGE alteration in course, such as to stem the tide when anchoring, or to enter, or proceed, after leaving a berth, or dock.
Way point	A mark or place at which a vessel is required to report to establish its position. (Also known as reporting point or calling-in-point.)

DANGERS IN THE USE OF VHF RADIO IN COLLISION AVOIDANCE

Notice to Owners, Masters, Skippers, Officers and Pilots of Merchant Ships, Yachts, Fishing Vessels and other Vessels fitted with VHF Radio Telephone Installations

1. The Department wishes to draw the attention of all concerned to the risks involved when VHF radio is used as a collision avoidance aid. In an increasing number of cases it has been found that at some stage before the collision VHF radio was being used by one or both parties in an attempt to avoid collision. The use of VHF radio in this role is not always helpful and may even prove dangerous.

2. Uncertainties can arise over the identification of vessels and the interpretation of messages received. At night, in restricted visibility or when there are more than two vessels in the vicinity the need for positive identification of the two vessels is essential but this can rarely be guaranteed. Even where positive identification has been achieved there is still the possibility of a misunderstanding between the parties concerned due to language difficulties however fluent they are in the language being used. An imprecise, or ambiguously expressed, message can have serious consequences.

3. Valuable time can be wasted while mariners on vessels approaching each other try to make contact on VHF radio instead of complying with the requirements of the Collision Regulations. There is the further danger that if contact has been established, identification has been achieved and no language or message difficulty exists, a course of action is chosen which does not comply with the Collision Regulations. This can lead to the collision it was intended to avoid.

4. The Department of Trade recognises that most ships are now fitted with VHF radio facilities* and are capable of bridge to bridge communication. Although the practice of using VHF radio as a collision avoidance aid may be resorted to on occasion, especially in pilotage waters, the risks described in this Notice should be clearly understood and the Collision Regulations complied with.

Department of Trade
Marine Division
London WC1V 6LP
May 1978

---

* Certain vessels are required to be fitted with a VHF radiotelephone when navigating in harbours, rivers and inland waterways of the United States (See Admiralty List of Radio Signals, Vol. 1.)

USE OF EMERGENCY POSITION INDICATING RADIO BEACONS (EPIRBs) AND HAND-HELD EPIRBs ON FREQUENCIES 121·5 MHz AND 243 MHz

Notice to Owners, Masters and Officers of Merchant Ships, Owners and Skippers of Fishing Vessels and Owners of Yachts

This Notice cancels M.863

1. Merchant Shipping Notice No. M.863 was issued in November 1978 and set out the Department of Trade's policy towards the carriage of EPIRBs and hand-held EPIRBs designed to operate on the frequencies 121·5 MHz and 243 MHz, which are used primarily for aeronautical purposes and which are an integral part of the aeronautical emergency system. The Department has reviewed this policy in the light of experience and information gained over the past two and a half years, and the policy contained in this present notice supersedes that contained in M Notice No. 863.

USE OF EPIRBs AND HAND-HELD EPIRBs AS HOMING AIDS

2. Small, lightweight EPIRBs and hand-held EPIRBs which operate on these frequencies and which can be carried on board ships and survival craft can be useful aids to the maritime Search and Rescue (SAR) services, primarily to assist SAR aircraft to locate units or persons in distress. Many of the UK SAR aircraft—and many of those operated by other national SAR services—are fitted with equipment which can identify signals from these beacons at distances of up to 100 miles and then home-in on them. The chances of these aircraft locating units or persons in distress will therefore be greatly improved where these beacons are used. The aircraft will not be constrained either by the prevailing conditions or by the size of the units in distress, as is the case with visual searches. The effectiveness of the homing equipment in the SAR aircraft may be seriously reduced, however, if there are several transmissions on the same frequency emanating from a limited sea area. Such a situation would have occurred if beacons had been activated by all those boats which were in distress in the 1979 Fastnet Race.

LIMITED ALERTING CAPABILITY

3. The beacons also have an alerting capability, but it is severely restricted. In most distress incidents, rapid assistance can best be provided by near-by shipping or, if this is not possible, by SAR units organised through the SAR services. However, neither ships nor the maritime watchkeeping facilities provided by HM Coastguard and the Post Office—the latter through their Coast Radio Stations—monitor the frequencies used by the

beacons. Therefore unless a distress incident occurs within a few miles of an aeronautical shore station monitoring 121·5 MHz and/or 243 MHz a beacon operating on these frequencies will need to rely on an overflying aircraft to receive the alert. The chances of that, however, are not good because of the pattern of aircraft routeing, the regularity of flights and the speed at which aircraft transit an area. Moreover, in the UK domestic flight information regions and on the North Sea and European routes, the pilots of most commercial aircraft monitor transmissions essential for the safe conduct of the flight and do not monitor 121·5 MHz unless specifically requested to do so by Air Traffic Control. Pilots of all aircraft on trans-atlantic flights do watch this frequency in the main Oceanic area, but the main purpose is to pick up an emergency call by another aircraft within range and to relay the message to the responsible Oceanic Control Centre on HF.

RECOMMENDATION

4. The Department of Trade therefore considers that EPIRBs and hand-held EPIRBs transmitting radio signals on the frequencies 121·5 MHz and 243 MHz are very useful aids to SAR aircraft searching for units or persons in distress, and that they are a useful supplement to conventional marine radio equipment operating on the international distress frequencies 500 kHz and 2182 kHz and on VHF Channel 16 (156·8 MHz). This conventional marine radio equipment is designed to ensure that the all-important distress alert will be received and can be acted upon quickly by those best in a position to help or arrange assistance. UK sea-going ships of 300 tons and above and fishing vessels of 12 metres or more in length registered in the United Kingdom are required to carry marine radio equipment by the Merchant Shipping (Radio Installations) Regulations 1980 and by the Merchant Shipping (Radio) (Fishing Vessels) Rules 1974 respectively. The Merchant Shipping (Life-Saving Appliances) Regulations 1980 and the Fishing Vessel (Safety Provisions) Regulations 1975 cover the carriage of radio equipment in survival craft. The Department of Trade, therefore, has no objections to these ships and vessels carrying types of beacons which the Home Office have found to be technically suitable for transmitting on the frequencies 121·5 MHz and 243 MHz (see paragraph 7 below) *in addition to* the statutory requirements for marine radio equipment. Similarly, the Department has no objections to such beacons being carried on small craft not covered by the Merchant Shipping and Fishing Vessel Regulations, but *strongly recommends* that such vessels carry conventional maritime radiotelephone equipment capable of operating on the international maritime distress frequencies 156·8 MHz (VHF Channel 16) or 2182 kHz *as well*.

THE IMPORTANCE OF CORRECT USE AND STOWAGE

5. It is very important that owners and potential users of these beacons are aware of the possible consequences of their misuse. First, they should

remember that the frequency 121·5 MHz is the frequency used by civil aircraft in an emergency and that it is possible that misuse or accidental activation of a beacon could mask a genuine alert by an aircraft in trouble. Secondly, they should remember that the SAR services have no way of telling whether or not the alert signal is genuine. Once these services are made aware of an alert they will respond but the resources they are able to call upon are expensive and may need to be diverted from genuine distress situations elsewhere. Repeated false alarms could easily bring these beacons into disrepute, which in view of their undoubted usefulness as homing aids would be most unfortunate.

6.   In distress situations therefore users should, wherever possible, first attempt to obtain assistance using conventional maritime radio equipment and procedures, and only activate their beacons if they are unable to obtain assistance by conventional means or when the SAR services request that they be activated in order to help SAR aircraft to locate them. Once activated, the beacons should not be turned off until the emergency is over. It is recommended that the beacons are stowed in the vicinity of the bridge in the case of merchant ships, in the vicinity of the wheelhouse in the case of fishing vessels and near to the helm in the case of yachts.

LICENSING

7.   In order to comply with Section 1 of the Wireless Telegraphy Act 1949, owners of EPIRBs and hand-held EPIRBs capable of operating on the aeronautical emergency frequencies must have them licensed by the Home Office. The Home Office will grant licences only in respect of those beacons which they consider to be technically suitable for transmitting on these frequencies and which meet the technical and performance standards laid down in the relevant Home Office specification. The beacons will be licensed only as voluntary equipment for carriage on board individual ships. Where these ships are required to fit conventional maritime radio equipment, the beacons will be licensed as an addition to and not a replacement for any of this compulsorily fitted equipment. Licensing will be effected by attaching a form of authorisation to the ship's licence. The use or installation of a beacon without a licence or otherwise than in accordance with the terms of the licence could lead to prosecution. The maximum penalties in the case of these radio beacons are a fine of £400 or up to three months imprisonment or both on summary conviction.

8.   Enquiries and applications concerning licensing and type-testing should be addressed to the Radio Regulatory Department, Home Office, Waterloo Bridge House, Waterloo Road, London SE1 8UA. A list of the beacons which have been found to be technically suitable for operating on the aeronautical frequencies 121·5 MHz and 243 MHz and which meet the Home Office technical and performance standards is available from the Home Office Radio Regulatory Department and from the Department's Marine Survey Offices.

USE OVERSEAS

9. It should be recognised that the UK may apply search and rescue arrangements different to some other countries. Therefore foreign vessels in UK waters and UK vessels in foreign waters may find that any locating devices they carry voluntarily for safety purposes may not be the most suitable.

CODE OF PRACTICE

10. A summary of the main points of this Notice is contained in the Annex.

Department of Trade
Marine Division
London WC1V 6LP
August 1981.

Important note: The Marine Division of the Department of Trade, which issues the Merchant Shipping Notices, is now known as the Department of Transport Marine Directorate, based at: Sunley House, 90 High Holborn, London WC1V 6LP.

EMERGENCY POSITION INDICATING RADIO BEACONS (EPIRBs) AND HAND-HELD EPIRBs OPERATING ON 121·5 MHz AND 243 MHz

CODE OF PRACTICE

1. The main function of these devices is as an homing aid in conjunction with SAR aircraft fitted with direction-finding equipment operating on these frequencies.

2. The devices have an alerting capability but it is limited and should not be relied upon. Commercial aircraft flying over the approaches to the United Kingdom within about 150 miles of the coast and over the North Sea do not normally keep watch on these frequencies. They do keep a watch on 121·5 MHz in Oceanic areas on trans-atlantic flights, although this watch is primarily for aircraft in distress.

3. Conventional maritime radio equipment is the best means of alerting near-by shipping and the maritime SAR services to a distress situation. Either of those is normally in the best position to help. Although the EPIRBs and hand-held EPIRBs operating on the aeronautical emergency frequencies are useful supplements to this equipment, they are not substitutes.

4. The carriage of EPIRBs and hand-held EPIRBs needs to be licensed. Only those devices which are technically suitable for operation on the aeronautical emergency frequencies will be licensed.

5. In order to protect the primary use of the frequencies—for civil aviation emergency purposes—and to avoid the misuse of the maritime SAR organisation, it is especially important that the devices are:

   (i) handled competently and neither dropped nor knocked;

   (ii) stowed appropriately (readily available should they be required but out of reach of unsupervised persons and so placed as to prevent accidental operation) and stored safely when in harbour.

6. Once activated, the devices should not be switched off until the emergency is over.

7. It should be noted that SAR aircraft will need to make special adjustments to their homing equipment when responding to transmissions on the same frequency from more than one vessel in a limited sea area.

Appendix V Phonetic Alphabet

Letter	Word	Pronunciation
A	ALFA	**AL** FAH
B	BRAVO	**BRAH** VOH
C	CHARLIE	**CHAR** LEE or **SHAR** LEE
D	DELTA	**DELL** TAH
E	ECHO	**ECK** OH
F	FOXTROT	**FOKS** TROT
G	GOLF	GOLF
H	HOTEL	HOH **TELL**
I	INDIA	**IN** DEE AH
J	JULIET	**JEW** LEE **ETT**
K	KILO	**KEY** LOH
L	LIMA	**LEE** MAH
M	MIKE	MIKE
N	NOVEMBER	NO **VEM** BER
O	OSCAR	**OSS** CAH
P	PAPA	PAH **PAH**
Q	QUEBEC	KEH **BECK**
R	ROMEO	**ROW** ME OH
S	SIERRA	SEE **AIR** RAH
T	TANGO	**TANG** GO
U	UNIFORM	**YOU** NEE FORM or **OO** NEE FORM
V	VICTOR	**VIK** TAH
W	WHISKEY	**WISS** KEY
X	X-RAY	**ECKS RAY**
Y	YANKEE	**YANG** KEY
Z	ZULU	**ZOO** LOO

Numeral	Pronunciation
0	ZERO
1	WUN

2	TOO
3	TREE
4	FOW-ER
5	FIFE
6	SIX
7	SEV-EN
8	AIT
9	NINER

Appendix VI   Glossary

ALL AFTER   Referring to part of a message after a certain word.

ALL BEFORE   Referring to part of a message before a certain word.

CORRECT   Message correct.

CORRECTION   Immediately previous part of the message is incorrect and will be repeated correctly.

DATE TIME GROUP   A group of six numerals representing the date and time that a message is sent. The first two represent the date, the remainder the time, e.g.: 1800 on the 25th August would be TWO FIVE ONE EIGHT ZERO ZERO.

IN FIGURES   Numerals written in figures.

IN LETTERS   Numerals written in phonetic letters.

I SAY AGAIN   I repeat the message.

SAY AGAIN   A request to repeat the message.

I SPELL   The following word or words will be spelled phonetically.

OUT   The end of the transmitting station's message.

OVER   The invitation to reply.

RADIO CHECK   A request for a check of clarity and signal strength of the transmission.

READ BACK   Read the message back.

RECEIVED   Message received.

SAY AGAIN   Repeat the message.

STATION   The term used for both ship and shore radio stations.

STATION CALLING   Used to answer a call when the identity of the calling station was not heard.

TEXT   The part of the radio telegram which follows is the text.

TRAFFIC   Any communication between stations.

THIS IS   Used before the identity of the station calling.

UNDERSTOOD   The message is understood.

WAIT   Indicating that the station called cannot immediately receive traffic.

WORD AFTER   The word after a specific phrase.

WORD BEFORE   The word before a specific phrase.

WRONG   The message is wrong.

Appendix VII   Mayday Procedure Form

IN CASE OF DISTRESS PROCEED AS FOLLOWS
1. Check the battery is switched on.
2. Switch on the radio and turn the power supply to maximum.
3. Select Channel 16.
4. Pick up the microphone, depress the PRESS-TO-TRANSMIT switch and send the following message slowly and distinctly:
   MAYDAY MAYDAY MAYDAY
   THIS IS YACHT . . . . . YACHT . . . . . YACHT . . . . .
   MAYDAY YACHT . . . .
   MY POSITION IS . . . .
   (Give the nature of the distress)
   I REQUIRE IMMEDIATE ASSISTANCE
   I HAVE . . . . PERSONS ON BOARD
   OVER
5. Release the PRESS-TO-TRANSMIT switch.
6. Wait for a reply.
7. If there is none, check the equipment and repeat the message.

KEEP THIS FORM NEXT TO YOUR VHF RADIO

Appendix VIII   Examination Centres

Address	Telephone Number
Southern	
College of Nautical Studies, Warsash,	
Southampton, Hants.	04895 6161
Isle of Wight	
National Sailing Centre, Arctic Road,	
Cowes, Isle of Wight.	0983 294941
South West	
Institute of Maritime Studies,	
Plymouth Polytechnic,	
Drake Circus, Plymouth PL4 8AA.	0752 264757
London	
City of London Polytechnic, School of Navigation,	
100, Minories, Tower Hill, London EC3N 1JY.	01-283-1030
East Anglia	
Lowestoft College of Further Education,	
Department of Maritime Studies,	
Herring Fishery Score, Lowestoft Suffolk.	0502 3259
Wales	
South Glamorgan Institute of Higher Education,	
Department of Maritime Studies,	
Western Avenue, Cardiff CF5 2YB.	0222 551111
Yorkshire and Humberside	
School of Engineering,	
Humberside College of Higher Education,	0482 224121
Queens Gardens, Hull, HU1 3DH.	ext. 283/200
Tyneside	
South Tyneside College,	
Department of Nautical Science,	

St. George's Avenue,
South Shields, Tyne & Wear. NE34 6ET   0632 560403

Scotland
RYA Scotland, 18 Ainslie Place,
Edinburgh EH3 6AU   031 226 4401

North West
Riversdale College of Technology,
Navigation Department, Riversdale Road,
Liverpool 19 3QR.   051 427 1227

Northern Ireland
School of Maritime Studies,
Ulster Polytechnic, Shore Road,
Newtonabbey, Co. Antrim BT37 0QB.   0231 65131

Jersey
VHF Radio Examinations, Highlands College,
P.O. Box 142, Jersey, C.I.   71065 ext. 354

Guernsey
College of Further Education, Route de Coutanchez,
St. Peter Port, Guernsey, C.I.   0481 27121

For Serving Servicemen
Examinations are administered by service
Sailing Associations.

ANSWERS TO QUESTIONS

1. The word MAYDAY.
2. MAYDAY MAYDAY MAYDAY
   THIS IS YACHT SPARROW YACHT SPARROW YACHT
   MAYDAY YACHT SPARROW
   MY POSITION IS ONE EIGHT ZERO START POINT ONE
   ZERO MILES
   I AM SINKING AND NEED IMMEDIATE ASSISTANCE
   I HAVE SEVEN PEOPLE ON BOARD
   OVER
3. SEELONCE MAYDAY.
4. By prefixing the message with the words MAYDAY RELAY.
5. a) Complete radio silence is no longer necessary and urgent messages
      can be passed.
   b) Radio silence is over.
6. Yes. It is correct.
7. MEDICO used after the urgency signal PAN PAN.
8. On a working channel after an initial announcement on Channel 16.
9. Channel 16 and then transfer to Channel 67.
10. Listen.
11. 06, 08, 72, 77.
12. It is required to do so.
13. a) No. It is for distress and calling only.
    b) One minute (preferably less).
14. No longer than 10 seconds.
15. Listen to the next traffic list.
16. On Channel 16 or direct on a working channel by prior arrangement.
17. No. The station's identity must always be used.
18. No. It is solely for use by the marina for marina business or by a
    yacht club for race organisation.
19. It is the primary intership channel.
20. Port operations.
21. Call the Coast Radio Station (on a working channel if appropriate),
    give your identity, state that you have been called on Selcall and
    request to be connected to the caller.
22. Listen on Channel 16 for any distress traffic. If nothing is heard, call
    the Coastguard on Channel 16, transfer to Channel 67 and tell the

Coastguard your position, what you have seen, and what action you are taking. The Coastguard will then assume responsibility for rescue co-ordination. If you cannot contact the Coastguard, try the Coast Radio Station. It is less complicated to pass the information ashore rather than initiate directly a Mayday Relay, particularly if details of the distress are unclear.

23. Call up Dover Port Control direct on Channel 74 and request permission to enter harbour.
24. Call up Dover Coastguard direct on Channel 10, give your position and inform the Coastguard that you are about to cross the Traffic Separation Scheme at right angles to the traffic flow.
25. Call Woolwich Port Radio direct on Channel 14, giving your identity, position and ETA at the Thames Barrier.

LIST OF ITEMS ON THE CASSETTE

The cassette contains examples of the following (in the order shown) together with an explanatory commentary.

Distress Call (Mayday)
Acknowledging a Distress Call
Mayday Relay
Imposing Radio Silence
Relaxing Radio Silence
Cancelling Radio Silence
Urgency Call (Pan Pan)
Requesting Medical Assistance
Making a Telephone Call
Contacting a Ship at Sea
Traffic Routeing
Selcall
Traffic List
Navigation Warning
Closing Down Radio Watch
Weather Forecast
Gale Warning
Coastguard's Small Boat Safety Scheme
Passage Report
Weather Report
Radio Check
Reporting in to the Port Radio Station
River Broadcast
Channel M
Intership Operation

INDEX